JUNE 2022

AN ANTHOLOGY OF ARTICLES

BRAIN BOOSTER ARTICLES

Contents

Preface

"Start writing, no matter what. The water does not flow until the faucet is turned on".

-Louis L'Amour

This book is a bouquet of articles contributed by students, professors and academicians. Hundreds of students and professors are contributing their work to Brain Booster Articles, we are here to provide ample information about Law and Contemporary issues. Our aim is to provide a platform for today's generation to express their views and ideas on law and contemporary law.

CHAPTER ONE

CRIME AGAINST WOMEN

Author: Alisha, IV year of B.A.,LL.B. from Hamdard Institute of Legal Studies and Research, Jamia Hamdard University

Abstract

Crime and violence are the most incessant crime against women occurring across the world. Physical and sexual abuse execute by husband or family members on women can have deep physical and psychological impact preventing the victim from ruling a normal life. Crime of such nature are persistent and extensively occurring in India. Low position of education and socio -economic background is a significant factor in domestic violence. One of the main reasons for crimes against women is the chiefly male dominated Indian society. In the face of laws to protect women from being victims of domestic violence, it is found that inequality which exists between gender, caste, class, sexual orientation and ability manifests itself in crimes against women. Stricter laws will help to reduce these crimes but this is not enough. what is required is social and cultural awakening to stop crimes against women.

Introduction

In the present situation, the violence and increasing crimes against women are seen by everyone around the world in some form or the other. This is indicating the enormity andseriousness of the demons committed against women in recent years. The global crusade for the extermination of violence against women is proof to this fact.The change in standard of living, lifestyle, imbalance in the economic growth, changes in social ethos and exiguous concern for the moral values contributes to a roguish outlook towards women due to which there is multiplication in crimes against women. Furthermore, such incidents are matter of solemnly concerns and its structure is absolutely necessary so that the women of India could live with respect, honour dignity, liberty and peace in an atmosphere free from beastliness, denigration and heinous crime.

Crime against women

The expression "crimes againstwomen" also knownas "violence againstwomen" or "gender – based violence" signifies fierce and actual demonstrations which are seriously coordinated towards women or girls. Any direct or indirect physical or mental torture to women or crimes in which women are victims are identified as crime against women.

"You can tell the condition of a nation by looking at the status of its women". This quote is given by Pt. Jawaharlal Nehru. It states that the conditions of women depict the social, economic & mental state of nation.

Crime against women in India is refer to physical, emotional or sexual assault carry out against women. It can be in the form of domestic violence, sexual harassment, acid attack, eve teasing, chain snatching, cybercrimes (bullying, abuse, violence, pornography), dowry deaths, staking, rape, and assault to outrage modesty. The main reason behind it gender discrimination which is present in our society. According to national crime record bureau (NCRB) 455 lakh cases registered against women and even more have not recorded that really makes our country India one of the most unsafe country for women.

There were more than 40%o of domestic violence cases in the lockdown phase due to covid 19 that's why the national commission for women (WCW) had to launch wats app number toreport these cases. Women are constantly facing and suffering from many threats like ranging from molestation forcible intercourse, harassment at workplace, carnal rape, domestic violence, and dowry system to honour killings. These are palpable crimes against women and due to covid 19 the situation has became worse than before that's why India also degraded at 140th rank in global gender gap report 2021 produced by world economic forum. As we know that India is male dominated society and due to male dominance, most of the women have been facing exploitation and oppression at every step oftheir lives.

Metropolitan are infamous for heinous crimes like rape and acid attack etc. for example Nirbhaya case of Delhi and Lakshmi Aggarwal case she is an India acid attack survivor, she was attacked in 2005 in new Delhi. For checking such crimes, pilot projects for 'safe city program' is launched by the government. There is one death every hour due to domestic violence because of dowry. To examine this, government came up with dowry prohibition act 1961 and domestic violence prevention act 2005. In the aftermath of 'kathua rape case' government came up with 'Protection of children against sexual offences (POSCO) act 2012 which aims to provide protection to children against sexual abuse.

There need to be more strict laws for protecting women, fast track courts also exist for crime against women, training centres should be opened for self-defence.

Crime againstwomen (glimpses of Indian penal code)

Kidnapping

The term abducting alludes to one or the other grabbing from India or capturing from legitimate guardianship. Sec 360 of the IPS states that whoever conveys any individual past India without his agree is said to capture that individual from India and whoever takes an away a minor (16yrs in the event of male and 18 yrs. if there should arise an occurrence of female) without his assent or the gatekeepers agree is said seize that individual from legitimate guardianship (sec 361). The discipline for this object is up to 7 year and fine. Sec 366 of IPS characterizes grabbing. Stealing or instigating lady to urge her marriage and strong sexual relations for which the guilty party can be rebuffed with detainment up to 10 years and fine.

Eve teasing

Eve Teasing is a code word utilized for public lewd behaviour or attack of women by men. It is an issue in the ongoing youth. A type of sexual hostility ranges in seriousness from sexual comments, brushing and whistles to grabbing. Sec 509 of the IPC states that whoever planning to affront the humility of any women, articulates any word, makes any sound or signal or displays any article which encroaches upon the protection of such woman will be rebuffed with detainment up to 3 years and fine.

Chain snatching

theft against women limits to chain-snatching and different resources. This is a typical issue of current culture. Advanced age ladies are the most impacted class of these wrongdoings. The wrongdoers likewise mask themselves as police authorities and request that ladies provide theirresources for the motivation of security. It is exposed to Sec 378 of IPC.

Rape

Rape is a lot more extensive term to be characterized and its degree is of more extensive viewpoint. It is the most considered normal wrongdoing against women and the Indianculture and framework has neglected to end this offensive wrongdoing. The world is considering India to be a country of rapist. The numbers have expanded immensely. The law framework has bombed absolutely. The offense can be sorted in different viewpoints as an assault of a minor girl, rape of woman (Sec 376), rape with murder (Sec 376A), rape in families, rape by community workers (Sec 376C), gang – rape (Sec 376 D), marital rapes (Sec 376B). The punishment for these offenses ranges from detainment up to 7 years to 20 years or Life detainment and also fine.

Domestic violence

Domestic violence at home is one more term which is normal in our country as women were and are viewed as the sub-par layers of human culture. The brain research was that the man procured and worked outside so he reserved the option to do anything with his significant other. Yet, with time, the pattern changed and presently women similarly work. These demonstrations of viciousness incorporate beating, rape, constrained sex and so on. Sec 498A of Domestic ViolenceAct, 2005 characterizes 1year punishment and fine. Cyber crimes

In the realm of innovation, India also had progressed itself in innovation and the ladies are an equivalent piece of it. Yet, the unhealthy personalities have not passed on any opportunity to affront women in the cyber world as well. There are a few cyber-crimes like bulling, abusing, pornography and so on which are going on every day against women. These violations have a few punishments under the Information Technology Act, 2000 which goes from detainment up to 3yearr to L.I. also, fine.

Dowry death

The malicious act of taking dowry in marriage is as yet normal in the rustic areas of India which whenever went against results to passings of women slowly. The quantity of suchpassings has expanded in the new year.

Acid attack

However, offer of acids without legitimate data have been prohibited by the public authority of India, Acid attack are still in pattern to compromise women and hurt them. Sec 326A and 326B of IPC states that whoever deliberately tosses corrosive for intolerable hurt or an attack will be rebuffed with imprisonment up to 7yrs to L.I. also, fine.

Stalking

Stalking is another wrongdoing in pattern against women. stalking means breaking the protection of women by following or normal contacts or checking on web or some other electronic correspondence. Whoever really does so will be rebuffed with imprisonment up to 3yrsto 5yrs and fine.

Assault to Outrage modesty

Whoever attacks or uses criminal power planning to outrageher modesty (1yr-5yrsdetainment) or stripping her or convincing her to be bare (3yrs-7yrs detainment) are obligated under Sec 354 and Sec354B individually.

Conclusion

Despite the quantity of regulations to secure and protect the privileges and premium of the ladies, the pace of wrongdoing against ladies and exploitation is expanding step by step. It is all around said that both partiesdeserve equal credit here. It suggests that main regulations are not dependable to manage and control the expansion of the violations against ladies in our general public. The concealment of hostile stares on ladies and teaching of social morals, ethics and values, regard and distinction in each person towards ladies is the need of great importance and is an enhancement factor that can similarly contribute in diminishing the quantity of violations against ladies. Notwithstanding, there is an exigency of additional severe and rigid regulations with the goal that any individual meaning to perpetrate such wrongdoings couldn't mess up the mental fortitude to act in assistance of hisaim.

Extreme penalty should be mandatory for heinous crimes like gang rape, acid attack, sexual assault, etc. the cases like Laxmi Aggarwal case, kathua kand and Nirbhaya gang rape put a question mark on women's right to live with dignity.

India, a country where women were worshiped as DEVI is today considered helpless and weak. Patriarchy has established that women are lesser to men and confined only to objects of pleasure and satisfaction. Regardless of these lawful arrangements and disciplines, India has still incapable to stop the savagery against women. women face these wrongdoings in all stages and in varying backgrounds. Assault has turned into a main issue in India because of expanding number of the wrongdoing. Following and retribution porn are at a high between the youthful grown-ups.From the above statistical data points, we can get a harsh thought that mindset of the general public needs an upset than any regulation or resolution.

Sex education in schools, proficiency among females, spreading mindfulness among individuals and a full stop to the man centric society is the answer for these wrongdoings. Aside from that, detailing of cases ought to be supported and the cases ought to be concluded inside a specified timeframe as postpone equity is no equity. The regulation additionally needs to move forward and change the regulations and genuine discipline ought to be given to the lawbreakers. Conjugal assault ought to be condemned as numerous crooks meander indiscriminately under the cover of marriage.

CHAPTER TWO

NO ONE'S RIGHT TO DETERMINE HER PRICE - DOWRY A CULTURAL CRIME

Author: Alina Sujith, I year of B.A.,LL.B.(Hons.) from The National University Of Advanced Legal Studies (NUALS), Kochi

ABSTRACT

Practices that prevail in the society under the masked disguise of tradition, custom, and religion are numerous. The concept of Dowry has evolved, being the root cause for heard and unheard stories of brutality, sexual violence, and death of lakhs and lakhs of women over the centuries. Even before the birth of a girl child, she is considered a burden due to the mental pressure the parents often carry to save for her marriage. This leads them to compromise her education and other areas of development—these restraints limit her world to the knot of a wedding chain attached with a price tag.

This article seeks to discover the origin of Dowry, how it deviated from its original intention of establishment in the colonial period and an analysis of the legal measures taken so far. The article goes on to cite judgments and their interpretation of cruelty as well. The gravity of a concept like Dowry is undermined and thus diluted into a widespread customary ritual associated with pride and prestige. Practices like female genital mutilation and Sathi were followed as obligations or as a part of customs. Just as we gradually realized how they are profoundly an infringement of one's rights and deeply life-threatening and limiting in nature, similarly, we need to work towards abolishing Dowry. This research highlights that it is high time we work against illogical practices that cripples humanity and exercise stringent legal measures.

DOWRY - A CULURAL CRIME – ANALYISIS

"Any young man, who makes dowry a condition to marriage, discredits his education and his country and dishonours womanhood." -Mahatma Gandhi

From discovering the gender of a girl child, an invisible boundary is drawn to presume capabilities, abilities, and even her future.Among the innumerous crimes committed against women, the one that attaches a price tag to a human being remains the most derogatory social evil, shattering one's self-worth and self-respect. While social evils have disguised themselves in the name of traditions, the practice of the Dowry system prevails even in the 21st century today. [i][ii]Dowry, by definition, means 'the money, goods, or estate that a woman brings to her husband or his familyin marriage'. The sad reality is that this is practiced even by the well-educated members of the society, who self – proclaim as progressive, ethical, and logical individuals. This calls for severe stringent measures to be exercised with no exceptions, and issues to be addressed from its root causes, to propagate conscious awareness and above all gain justice to women who have been the victims of the unimaginable tortures and sufferings as a result of these customary practices that stubbornly resists change.

The discriminatory practices against women have prevailed since time immemorial, but the practice of the dowry system, in particular, cannot be traced back to ancient India.[iii] In ancient texts, there is a reference of 'Yautraka', a material gift that confirms two people joined in matrimony. The dowry system can be seen in the Vedic period, where the gifts from parents and relatives were considered the women's property or possession called 'Stridhan'.[iv]Dowry was initially developed as a system established by women to support women. It was initiated to provide financial independence to women even after marriage, and the bride's family provided for the same.[v]In pre-colonial India, this system was a resort to women in cases of emergency and served as a tool for their independence. The principal difference here is that wealth or valuables were given to the bride and not the groom or their family. Where did we take this steep turn where the system initiated to provide a resort to women translated to be the reason for inflicting mental and physical torture, sexual violence, oppression, and even dowry murder?During the establishment of the feudal or Zamindari system, the British completely prohibited women from possessing any land or property, and her wealth would now belong to her husband. This later became a matter of prestige and a ground for greed to inherit wealth. Women continued to bear the sufferings of the patriarchal society, and marriage transformed into business deals or a source of earning wealth.

Here let us analyse some legal measures taken in order to prevent and abolish this practice.[vi]In 1975, the earliest protest against dowry took place in Hyderabad, headed by a female-led progressive organization. In 1980's New Delhi,human rights activist Satyarani Chadha became the face of the Anti- dowry movement. [vii]The Dowry Prohibition Act was established in 1961 states that 'If any person, after the commencement of this Act, gives or takes or abets the giving or taking of dowry, he shall be punishable with imprisonment for a term which shall not be less than five years, and with the fine which shall not be less than fifteen thousand rupees or the amount of the value of such dowry'. [viii]This was amended twice in 1984 and 1986 and was followed by the Dowry Prohibition Rules,1985. Even after these legal measures, there was no significant relaxation in this practice. [ix]In the cases of G.V. Siddaramesh v. State of Karnataka and Gananath Pattnaik v. State of Orissa,the judgments stated that cruelty could not be reduced to a single definition, as harm inflicted could be mental or physical and the concept of the same will vary from person to person. Section 304 B of the Indian Penal Code defines dowry death and [x]according to NCRB, nearly 7,000 dowry deaths were reported in the year 2020 in India.

India's most literate state, Kerala witnessed three suspicious dowry deaths of – Vismaya, Archana, Suchithra; this incited sparking conversations and led to introspections about moral responsibility as members of a society.Such is the tragic irony of fate that a female requires to turn into a justice hashtag to draw attention to pertaining social injustices. Stringent measures and proper implementation of laws are the only recourse, along with a refreshed perception of marriage, gender roles, and the position of women in a family. These concepts can save society from the pitfalls of social evils and develop a generation conscious enough to distinguish and work towards abolishing crimes such as dowry that hang a price tag on women, whose value is beyond.

CHAPTER THREE

CRITIQUE OF PRESS REGULATION IN INDIA

Author: Moksh Bhatnagar, III year of B.B.A.,LL.B.(Hons.) from Unitedworld School of Law, Karnavati University

Freedom of Press

In any democracy, the free exchange of ideas and knowledge takes place when there is unrestricted communication. It is guaranteed through the "freedom of speech and expression", the most cherished fundamental right, as envisaged not only under the Constitution of India[i], but various international covenants[ii], resolutions, and international legislations. In any democracy, communication- oral, pictorial, or musical communication of speech- is an essential right involving people to contribute to civic activities. However, the whole idea of having the freedom of speech and expression is pointless if such communication and speech are "locked" in boxes than openly shared without fear. The media in any democratic country plays a major role in circulating such speeches and expressions. It shall be duly noted that freedom of speech and expression includes freedom of propagation of ideas and that freedom is ensured by freedom of circulation.[iii]

Although there is no separate constitutional provision for the freedom of the press in the constitution, it is implicit under Article 19(1)(a). The same has been established and reiterated by the Supreme Court on several occasions[iv]. Hence, it is inherent that the role of media is of utmost importance in any democracy. The media is popularly referred to as the "Fourth Estate"[v] as it plays a crucial role in a democracy. It is the watchdog of public interest and its role as witness and commentator on the activities of the Government, various social and political institutions, and society at large, is vital. As the voice of the masses, representing their concerns, the media not only interprets and comments on the present but also sets the agenda for the future.

The Supreme Court has further held in the landmark case of the Cricket Association of Bengal[vi]has observed the following:

"...One-sided information, disinformation, misinformation and non-information all equally create an uninformed citizenry which makes democracy a farce when the medium of information is monopolised either by a partisan central authority or by private individuals or oligarchic organisations... Hence to have a representative central agency to ensure the viewers' right to be informed adequately and truthfully is a part of the right of the viewers under Article 19(1)(a).

The principle of media pluralism has been recognised as it can be logically inferred from such observations. Any effort to erode the plurality of voices in media will be a direct violation of Article 19(1)(a) of the Constitution.

Issues in the current regulation

Currently, there are no restrictions for investment in the press, or any such funding rules, however, there is a limit of 26% Foreign Direct Investment which is only allowed through government-approved routes.[vii] The non-regulation of who can own or fund press and media houses is a significant hurdle to free and "unadulterated" speech and opinions of the press. The commercialisation of the press and media seem to have hurt editorial independence. During times of struggle for independence, newspapers and press was a medium to imbibe the feeling of patriotism and to display resilience against the colonial powers. Since then, the press has evolved on a completely different tangent.

To regulate the press, upon the recommendations of the First Press Commission, the Press Council was established in 1965[viii] and further administrative amendments were constituted in 1978[ix]. The Press Council was established not just to regulate the press but to perform a variety of functions which included concerning itself to matters of concentration of ownership which may hamper the freedom of the press. Section 13 (2)(i) of the Press Council Act reads as follows:

(i) “to concern itself developments such as concentration of or other aspects of ownership of newspapers and news agencies which may affect the independence of the Press;”

Hence, it is well established that the press council has the extensive authority to take into account whenever any ownership and funding rules impede the functioning of the press. However, the Press Council is merely a statutory body with no punitive powers. It may draw recommendations but as no authority to impose punishments, making it a toothless tiger. The same has been duly noted in the case of Ajay Goswamivs Union of India[x]. It was submitted that the Press Council was a body that was constituted for preserving the freedom of the press and maintaining and improving the standards of newspapers and news agencies is a powerless body. Hence, even though there exists an authority in pages of legislation, its presence is almost negligible. The Press Council has no jurisdiction on imposing restrictions on ownership.

The direct or indirect ownership/funding of the press by the government may have ruinous effects on the functioning of a democracy. Even though the media interests of corporate entities have usually been justified on the grounds of the funds they bring to this capital-intensive sector and the right to invest in a line of business of their choice, a quid pro quo deal with the media entity guaranteeing favourable coverage can seldom be ruled out.[xi] Hence, the freedom of the press may not just be compromised, but the same press and media may even be used as an instrument of self-promotion during electoral campaigns. Unrestricted ownership and the overweening commercialisation of the media has compromised the media's primary objective and responsibility of fair and unbiased news dissemination, thereby severely affecting its credibility.

Impact of such fallacies

The absence of competent regulatory framework has had dire implications on the status on the press of India. The lack of rules and regulations of the mediation of the press, and further, there is no punitive body for the violations of any rules or regulations, has deteriorated the situation of press. The freedom of press, which the Press Council of India vows to protect, has been destroyed by the inaction and lack of authority of the Press Council. The following has been duly noted through the following occurrence:

Reliance Industries (RIL) acquired complete controlling stake in Network18 for a whopping amount of Rs. 4000 crores. Upon such acquisition, senior journalists as the likes of RajdeepSardesai and SagarikaGhose gave in their resignations, with Sardesai indicating the compromise of editorial independence as a reason for his resignation.[xii] Further, there were several anonymous complaints about the change in the professional behaviour at Network18. For instance, ex-employees testified that they were pressurised to cover the loss of AamAadmi Party and ArvindKejriwal, who had been launching attacks against Mr Mukesh Ambani. The media house has denied all these allegations.[xiii]

Further, there are no regulations or funding rules for the press. This implies that press houses can obtain funds from any source, domestic or foreign. Adulteration of content is a common phenomenon in such conditions. There may be foreign entities that acquire a stake in editorial boards due to their financial influence on the press house, and satisfy their own propagandas, compromising editorial freedom and ethical standards of the media. For instance, China has allegedly funded a media house named NewsClick, as a probe by the Enforcement Directorate revealed that the media house received an amount of about Rs 38 crores in order to promote their propaganda and interests through the peddling of fake news. There are also several allegations against the media house concerning money laundering.[xiv]

Recommendations and Conclusions

Beyond any doubt, the press in the country certainly needs saving, saving in the form of regulation. The current status of freedom of the press is at the lowest point possible. The current self-regulatory framework has drastically failed not just the freedom of the press, but the profession of journalism as a whole. It is beyond doubt that a profession, which is as important to the functioning of a country as the press is, needs to be regulated.

The principle of self-regulation entails regulation by itself where the media does not have a regulatory body under it. There comes the dilemma of who maintains the checks and balances in what is written and published. Theoretically speaking, leaving the regulation to the media itself would generate the likelihood that it may subjugate regulatory aims to its own business goals.

It is indeed time that there is a uniform code of conduct for journalists, members of the press and even the stakeholders in the press. It can be concluded that if the government believes in self-regulation, it should have taken efforts to mandate or facilitate the coming together of the broadcasting fraternity under one umbrella. It should have formalised the self-regulatory code and penalties by consensus and by giving some sort of legal recognition for the decisions of self-regulatory bodies and thereby limiting the applicability of extant laws and by prescribing some minimum standards to be followed by them in the interests of viewers.

It is a fact that no human activity is feasible without some form of control. No institution can work progressively if it is self-regulated. Primary to self-regulation is the theory of intended conformity. The self-regulatory bodies cannot function unless it is free from bureaucracy, industrial and particular interests; unless a random check is done within the institution; unless it has the authority to oblige moral permit, for instance, the publication of rectification or an asking for forgiveness. In the light of these, it needs to be scrutinized as to how far self-regulation for media is justified. Therefore, the assumption is that just leaving the regulation to the media itself would create the possibility that it may subvert regulatory goals to its own business goals.

CHAPTER FOUR

RIGHT OF CHILDREN ARE RIGHTS FOR FUTURE

Author: Nayan Patel, II year of B.B.A.,LL.B.(Hons.) from Christ University

Abstract

The Republic of India is a country in South Asia having 29 states, its capital being New Delhi. The republic of India contains a lot of diversity in its custom, tradition, and even in languages out of which Hindi Is the most used language. It has a population of about 1.21 billion, having 2 largest population and the seventh most extensive country in the world. It is a vast country and also among the developing countries in the world. Despite this fact, the country has shown remarkable progress in the economy with an average of 7.3% over the past five years. But the inequality is still reflected in the country in the low human development attainments of the country's most marginalized groups including cast, tribal and rural population, women, transgender people living with HIV, and migrants. Although India has made a lot of efforts to counter the social and legal issues of the country, they seem to be uneven. India's children continue facing some of the hardest situations anywhere in the world, with high malnutrition rates, child labor and forced begging, and childhood illnesses such as diarrheal diseases.

Introduction

We have read about child rape and child sexual exploitation in the papers daily. India leads the world as a country with maximum cases of child exploitation. Even the parents of sexually abused children are too scared to tell anyone because of the fear of being ashamed in society. Somewhere there is the fault of the society also they should take the matter with concern rather than taking it as a shameful act. And it is not true that the act is committed only by the stranger but many times it is committed by the members of the family, relatives, and even the neighbors. According to the survey, in 90% of the cases, the children are exploited by the person with whom they know and trust. Many cases have come forward where the father, uncle, or neighbors have sexually exploited the children. In this situation, one can say that they need protection at home also. They are many times afraid to mention this because of fear of not knowing what has occurred. Sexual exploitation Is not rape alone. There can be many forms of sexual exploitation like clicking nude photos of children, making children watch pornographic content, physically teasing them, etc. this type of activity creates an impact on the children throughout their life and make them fearful, worried, guilty, and lonely. Can be defined in other words also Sexual exploitation refers to actual or attempted abuse of vulnerabilities, discriminatory powers, or trusting positions committed against children and families served by volunteers for sexual purposes. Sexual abuse is the actual or threatened physical assault of a sexual nature, whether violent, unequal, or compulsory, committed by a volunteer against a child or family member serving.

There are many religious and cultural practices are going on in India even today

A. Female Genital Mutilation

It means the removal of the part of the total removal of the external female genitalia organ for non-medical uses. The practice does not have any health benefits for girls and women. And it is mostly practiced in young girls between the age of infancy and the age of 15 years. The practice is a gross violation of the human rights of girls and women. It showcasesthe inequality between the sexes and the extreme form of discrimination against young girls and women. It forbids the person's right to health, security, and physical integrity and also the right to be free from torture and cruel, inhuman, and degrading human treatment, and the right to life.

B. Self- flagellation

Temporarily relieving mental distress by repeated use of non-lethal methods that cause socially unacceptable injuries in the dermis and epidermis is physical harm to oneself. The area selected for self-destruction is easily hidden by clothing without implying inaccessibility.

Some causes of self-flagellation

1. Because of traumatic events
2. Disorders
3. Anxiety disorder

C. Baby tossing

This ritual is followed in some parts of Indiafor 700 years by both the Hindu as well as the Muslimgroup of people. In this ritual, the infant or small babies are thrown from the roof of the temple by the priest and about 14-15 men are standing down with the blanket to catch the baby, and men surrounding them are charged to hand over the babies to the readily waiting mother. They perform this ritual with the belief that the health of the child will be good and to shower the good luck and because of this dangerous act the child takes a long time to come out of this shock or trauma.

Child labor

As India is gaining the power to become the world's future monetary superpower it is very important to securer the people of the nation, which are without a doubt the children of the nation. Child labor which is prohibited in the constitution of India is still practiced widely in India. India has the greatest number of child laborers (less than 14 years) in the world about 100-150 million out of 44 million are occupied with hazardous jobs.

Crimes against children

The National crime bureau (NCRB) released the statistics from the 2020 report that there is a sharp rise in the crime against children physically as well as sexually also. There is also a rise in the cases recorded under the Protection of children under the sexual offense (POSCO) act. With the technology getting the advent the crime against children also getting new faces as Online bullying, molesting the child, coral punishment, and physical violence against them in school and family. The pandemic has been proved to the cheery on the cake as it exacerbated the other existing pandemic like malnutrition, poverty, violence, and mental health issues.

Intoxicating a child

The hunger of a child can end up in different ways like he can be the target of the sex racket or may end up being a beggar or many a time because of hunger and many other reasons the children may start consuming the intoxicating substance like cigarettes, alcohol and make them intoxicated to escape them from the reality and make them slavery work and many other types of the illegal work. They are even used to traffic the drugs from one place to another as being children they can not be suspected easily by the cops and they take advantage of this and use them to transport drugs and many other drugs, alcohol, etc.

Child prostitution

Prostitution in easy language means to deliver the sexual service in exchange for money or monetary benefit. The children are forced to deliver the sexual service and even not taken their consent and the age for giving consent is different in different countries e.g. the age of giving consent is 14 years in Italy and India it is 18 years. Nevertheless, the offenses like kidnapping, abducting, and all other child-related offenses are usually covered or related to child prostitution. Although there is much legislation across the globe to stop child prostitution it prevails due to a large number of pedophiles in society.

Child Rights in India

A human being below the age of 18 years is a child unless, under the law applicable to the child, the age of majority is attained earlier. The future of the nation depends on the growth and well-being of the children of the nation. They are considered the assets of the nation. The state must protect and look after the children and achieve this goal the state must grant certain rights to the children. Many laws and regulations are made after signing the United Nations Convention on the right of the child also known as CRC 1989 and India was also a signatory of the convention. However, it was ratified in India on 11 December 1992. It also has the preamble setting out of different principles the CRC is built upon.

Part 1 (article 1-41) sets the rights of the children and the obligation of the governments and many rights such as Survival Rights, Development Rights, Protection Rights, Participation Rights, and many more.

Part 2 (Article 42-45) talks about the provisions regarding the implementation of the provisions of the CRC

Part 3 (Article 46-54) Includes the Provision for signing the convention and also states the rules and regulations for Ratification, enforceability, amendment, denouncement, etc of the convention

Also, the government has taken timely measures on the same, and some of the important and effective legislation and schemes are The Children and adolescent (Prohibition and Regulation) Act, 1986 and Child Labour Project Scheme (NCPL) Scheme.

The Children and adolescent (Prohibition and Regulation) Act, 1986

This act has implied strict provisions against child labour section 3 of the act states that the child should not be employed in a hazardous occupation except the family business. Also, he/she can be employed in the Audio-Visual Entertainment industry within safety measures. The Central Government appointed the technical body to lay down the guidelines

Also, the Act states the limited work hours along with the holidays to the children and the employer should send the notice to the inspector regarding the working of the child Section 13 directs the employer to maintain the proper health condition in the workplace.

It is a successful piece of legislation as it has done a remarkable job by lying down the norms, which industry s hazardous for the children, and which are not. Also rehabilitating the children who suffered from child labour and the chance of returning them to the mainstream society.

National Child Labour Project Scheme

This is initiated by the Ministry of Labour and employment in 1988. The ministry took the survey of child labour and sent them to the special school with the vocational training, a bridge course Mid-day meal, and also a stipend of rupees the 150 per month. The members of the committee were withdrawn from the reputed NGOs, concerned government departments, and panchayats. The scheme was able to solve the problem to some extent. Formal education can solve the root cause of child labour because the educated child will have less chance of falling prey to child labor.

M.C. Mehta VS State of Tamandu&Ors.

In this case, the eminent environment lawyer M.C Mehta has fileda Writ petition on the Apex Court stating that there is a gross violation of article 24 in the Shivkasi where children below the 14 years of age are employed in the factory or mine or any other hazardous activates. The committee of the advocates was appointed and a detailed report was presented to the state government after the proper analysis of the situation the Court directed the guidelines in favor of the children below 14 years of age to be employedand the work condition and also the period of the work is limited. Not only in shivkasi but there is the problem of child labour in many parts of the nation not only in India. And it can be solved by the joint efforts of the State as well as the Central Government and through various articles like Article 24, 39, 39(e), 39(f), 41,45,47 it is possible and the judgment also mentions thatIndia's commitment towards the Convention of Child Rights which was earlier adopted in UNGA in 1989.

The Protection of Children from the Sexual Offenses (POCSO) Act, 2012

This act provides the conclusive definition of the term "penetrative sexual assault" and "aggravated penetrative sexual assault". The act gives proper punishment to the person who commits the crime of sexual assault on a child below the 16 years of the age then a minimum of 20 years of the imprisonment and may be extended to the life imprisonmentand the compensation should be provided for the rehabilitation and the medical expenses for the victim. The act also made strict provisions on the sharing of child pornography and making an obscene gesture to the child. This act encourages the people to come forward and let their voices be heard by the world. There have been significant increases in the number of cases in the court of the law and also the higher conviction rate. The main problem which was faced earlier was the lack of awareness but the act has relevant provisions for that also the people were made aware of the provisions and the consequences they might face for the violation of the laws. So, after analysis of the act, one can say that is it very much effective in the arena of child sexual abuse.

Juvenile Justice

Many times, if children commit a serious offense, they are considered an adult during the trial and they did not get the proper protection that they are entitled to and this becomes an international debate. Juvenile justice came into existence because the mind of the children is easily manipulated to commit serious crimes and has been seen as dead in the Nirbhaya Gang Rape Case in Delhi. The accused was just a few months short of 18 years. And this made the juvenile justice act which replaced the existing law and ensured that the juveniles between the age group of 16-18 years can also be treated as an adult in a court of law if they commit serious offenses. And this creates the ambiguity between the children and the juvenile and the rights of the juveniles has become a concern for many countries and many guidelines have been passed like the Beijing rules, Riyad guidelines, Havana guidelines, and Vienna Guidelines. And after that, the Indian legislation has also passed the Juvenile Justice (care and protection of children) Act,

2015. Under this act, it establishes the Board consisting of the reputed Civil servant and the social activists in the board dealing with the juveniles in the issue. Through Section 4 of the Act. This act shows the amount of leniency towards the juveniles in a matter of arrest, detention, and also the Bail and also the psychological test of the juvenile is done who commits the serious the crime. The committee also adopts the child from the parents who can not maintain their child. The special guideline for rehabilitating is also mentioned under Section 39 of the Act. The Juvenile Justice (care and protection of children) Act, 2015, since its inception has done a remarkable job in the field of the juvenile rights and protection and has been proved as a cherry on the cake by keeping the NCPCR in charge of implementation will ensure the proper implementation of the act. Which proved necessary for the success of the act.

SampurnaBehrua vs UOI

Through this landmark judgment the honourable justice Madan. B. Lokur criticized the government for not properly ensuring the rights of the juvenile justice act and also directed to fill the vacancies of the NCPCR and SCPCR to have enough manpower and directed that not using the shelter homes for the children is a clear violation of the article 21 of the Indian Constitution. And also a request was made to every state High Court tomake a child-friendly court in every state.

Right to education

Education is a powerful weapon that can change the world stated by Nelson Mandela and education is an integral part of the development of the child. The right to free education is guaranteed under Article 21A of the Indian Constitution which is also a fundamental part of Part 3. It orders the state that children under the age of 14 years should be provided free and compulsory education in such a manner that the state may determine by law and it is also backed by the Right of Children to Free and Compulsory Education Act, 2009. The government has initiated my scheme for making primary education accessible to all the children remotely the scheme is like Sarva Shikha Abhiyan and also the Beti Bachao Beti Padhao.

Conclusion

The legislative, The Executive,and the Judiciary are the wings that are constantly making efforts since independence to protect the child's rights as their national asset. The legislation has taken timely steps to protect the rights and made necessary provisions as and when needed to make the proper laws and regulations. The Executive has made sure that the laws are followed in all the regions of India which has the 2 largest populations in the world. Although laws are there it has been difficult to implement them and ensuring the development, survival, protection and normal growth of the children is a continuous process. The Judiciary also made a timely decision and the proper judgment is made in favor of the children's rights the main focus is given to the situation of the children and the proper environment fortheir growth is maintained. After reviewing all the things there is an imminent need to increase the allocation of the resources.

As we get to know through this that there is a need to improve the certain condition of the child'srights and it is the duty of the state to protect it as they too have the right to a dignified life. Children being the assets of the nation the country cannot grow without building its foundation. Many times the parents and the legal heirs are not aware of the rights of the children and they suffer in silent.

CHAPTER FIVE

RIGHT TO FREEDOM OF EXPRESSION AND INTERNET CENSORSHIP IN INDIA: A CRITICAL STUDY

Author: Rayma Simran. C, LL.B. from CMR University

ABSTRACT

The Indian Constitution has guaranteed freedom of speech and expression to the citizen of India under Article 19(1)(a) to let out their view and opinion towards any matte. It includes political view about the government and there representatives. On other hand in the contemporary times the internet has become a major part of Indian society that has given a Wider of platform to the citizen to give there view upon any of the issues, at the same time the internet usage are been subjected to censorship and controlled by government which is under reason restriction guaranteed by the constitution under Article 19 (2).

The growth of internet has brought a fastest way of accessing All kind of information and easily connect the people to share information millions of people in a country are using this network as a tool to express their opinion on different matters. In this research paper it mainly focuses upon the concept of Right to freedom of expression and internet censorship in India. And it also explains online censorship elaborately that why internet censorship is required in today's period and how individuals freedom and censorship has been explained in the judicial pronouncement.

Keywords: Freedom of speech and expression, Censorship, Internet Censorship in India

RESEARCH METHODOLOGY

The research aims to set out a cognitive studywhich is conceptual in nature and this paper is purely based on the Doctrine research and this study is referred as a secondary source study only not the primary source which directly include the raw materials as interview in with people and taking the survey which was not possible, what's possible only to collect secondary source the facts and figures have been referred from various official websites, blogs and the required information gathered from different articles books and research papers, news etc..

RESEARCH OBJECTIVES

The study helps to understand the purpose of internet censorship under the context of India

It elaborate the major reasons of censorship of internet

Internet censorship and its challenges in recent periods and, including Internet censorships pros and cons

RESEARCH QUESTIONS

Whether internet censorship is necessary in recent period ?

Whether internet censorship create an issue on free speech and free flow of information ?

HYPOTHESIS

When Constitution of India provided right to freedom of expression it is not an absolute right where as the same constitution is also provided reasonable restriction. In the same context internet censorship as also been a part it, which is necessary for the present era but it can also be negatively used by government in an political agenda, as a result it can affect the third pillar of democracy which is media.

LITERATURE REVIEW

Vani Agrawal, Priyanshi Sharma, Internet Censorship in India

This article elaborate term internet censorship in India with the help of various tools and method used for censoring the internet in India it also looks into each and every mode of censorship internet from the user since 1999 to 2013 and gives an elaborate report of internet statistic it also mainly focus is appoint the concept of internet censorship under Indian context[1].

Suman Pathak and Aakanksha Derashree, Internet Censorship in India: Boom or Bane[2].

This article the researcher into discuss about the battle between freedom of speech and expression and internet sensation the discussion widely focus upon online censorship which involves politics and other corruption practices in large it also discuss about the policy agenda towards restriction under freedom of speech.

Garima Saxena, Issue of Censorship in India

This block post analyses the challenges faced by internet censorship in India and

Recognize the legal system of various countries such as United State of America Sweden and United Kingdom about the freedom of speech and expression and it demonstrate the Indian Constitution freedom of expression to give an idea throughout media law[3].

Sarthak Dash Bhatta Amishra, Right to Access to Internet in India: Fundamental Rights or a Glorified Privilege[4]?

In this article there is a analyze the contemporary times where internet has become a part of Indian society and clarified the questions regarding right to access internet whether it is a privilege or a fundamental rights moreover does right to access internet is protected under Article 21.

Devanshree Rai and Gitika Jain, Internet Censorship: Misuse of the Freedom of Speech and Expression[5]

In this web article the writer express is view on misuse of the freedom of speech and expression in the context of internet censorship it also discuss about the reasonable restrictions and social media battles for is reckless use of free speech.

Raagya Priya Zadu, Internet censorship[6]

This block post discusses about the internet censorship and analysis if internal censorship is the freedom of speech and expression being as a disadvantage or is Internet the new platform to look through the words largest democracy.

Koustubh Chandra, Necessity of Censorship of Internet[7]

In this web article the author Express about the various aspect of internet censorship in India which also includes its Pro and cons and The article basically give the basic recommendation for the government to implement the policy and planning about the various stages taken for censoring internet.

Chandrima Mitra, Social media norms must balance freedom of speech, censorship[8]

In this article it talks about the facts that most popular social media platforms are always based on US whether it might effect the order of executives on such social media platform in USA does this create an impact globally it has been balanced and discussed in this article and article majorly focus upon censoring social media content and the right to freedom of speech how Indian codes have repeatedly deal with it

INTRODUCTION

The internet across the Global one of the fastest growing Technology in terms of technology are avarying degree that has been reflected and still it will continue to reflect the evolution of freedom on the way of recent technology and advance network connections the Ambit of freedom as being substantiallyheated up and reached when another stage[9]. The expression of freedom can also be more suitable to suggest that a technology which has been used not just by in Individual for an a pleasant or Unpleasant intention but also for moderate regime, for the more in an diverse society a public policy should always be director for the purpose of promoting and expanding the liberty of the citizen this act as a technical tool the usage of technology.

Internet as a largest public platform due to it's availability and accessibility there are wider audience. Internet which is used for the purpose of sharing information helps in providing various opportunities so basically it becomes a medium which can be used in the term it has to be protected for the purpose of preventing crimes[10]. The prevention measures a concept of internet censorship, internet censorship is an control over the axis viewed or published data on the Internet platform. Internet censorship is governed and controlled by government and it can also carried out by an public organisation for any purpose that act as a preventive measure against individual religious business or moral reasons and the purpose of the censorship is to protect the society from defamation, invasion of privacy and other illegal business to carry out.

It is said that " Any art that could corrupt morality should be censored"[11] under this context under article 19 of the Indian Constitution right to freedom of speech and expression which is a fundamental right is applicable on the same way with the reasonable restriction is also being mentioned where the scrutinity comes in the form of censorship, the conflict between right to freedom of expression and censorship is always Debatable concept because when the freedom of expression give the right to express a individuals free opinion the censorship try to scrutinize and limit there rights in view point of the conflict.

The Main Purpose of Internet Censorship

To access internet is one of the easiest and fasters method internet has been easily available for everyone to have access that all the data available on the Internet provides various information's, running businesses moreover, multinational companies are sustained due to internet in such case in the present day internet Usage also have demerits such as easily available access to internet can distract meaning teenagers time and talent moreover it is widely open for the adults world it is necessary for the peoples to share their opinion in any of the platform in the internet but at the same time it can also create a greater disaster if it leads the youth towards illegal activity and the opinion related to field like politics, arts, entertainment, sports and philosophy or always has negative and positive impact. Internet Censorship act as a preventive method for the public and the society to follow the social norms it is necessary to handle the situation which comes under defamation against state and any illegal business, invasion of privacy etc.

The most common reasons for internet censorship are:-

- Protecting national security such as using internet for buying weapons illegal drugs it also prevents from the terrorism.
- In the concerned of protecting minors from abuse firms of human trafficking violence drugs pornography.
- To protect human dignity, prevent the individual from incitement towards hate speech, racial hatred, creating enmity, discrimination.
- Protecting from economic security such as Fraudulent activity Duplicate Credit Cards.
- Protecting Information and Communication from hacking
- Protection of privacy such as unauthorized communication from any individuals personal data protection of the repetitions from deformation and unlawful comparative advertising.
- Protection from unauthorized distribution of any copyrighted materials under intellectual property.

Internet Censorship under Freedom of Expression

The freedom of speech and expression provided under article 19(1)(a) is not an absolute right where as it involves reasonable restrictions which is provided the same constitution under 19(2). The censorship issue is a debatable topic in India the censorship issue as been worried by citizen whether it might effect there free speech supporters and civil rights, where the Indian government over the past years have been tried to sensor free the speech and free flow of the information and communication, in the form of right to freedom of speech and expression which act as a fundamental rights under article 19(1)(a) of Indian Constitution when It Up held a basic right by the constitution various judgement has been dead to express the application of reasonable restriction with the help of Supreme Court judgements.

Implementation of reasonable restriction which act as a limitation that it post on each and every citizen of a country to enjoy the rights these restriction are always conserve as useful the different period why the government in contest of free speech an expression in the recent period the reason amendment took place on 2019 was The Unlawful Activity (Prevention) Act 1967 under this act amendment to please that altered section 35 of the act and give power to the central government to notify any individual if he involved in terrorism prayer to this act the government can protect the interest of the state it's sovereignty and integrity[12], in such case freedom of speech and expression as become a medium of interest in an Central part of article 19(1)(a) under Indian Constitution for the more any restriction for the same in accordance with the article 19 2 of the constitution in the contest of internet censorship is taken seriously by the Indian government at the state and also Central even National level[13].

Issues and Necessity of Internet Censorship

Cyber censorship was the first establishment by parliament in the information technology act which leader foundation Framework towards rules and regulation to use or access the internet for communication security trade and hacking etc. The main purpose of this act is to provide protection towards axis of internet and also a legal recognition for the transaction that has been carried out by in the means of electronic device with the help of internet in the letter period it has been amended the Indian penal code[14] and also other act such as Indian Evidence Act[15] and Reserve Bank of India[16] act for the other matters which involved security purpose.

Government by introducing various amendments in the hack as successfully censored free speech and flow of information in such case 2008 and abundant of act also give over towards the government to censor the content or data, to protect the sovereignty and integrity of the country such as defence of India and the security of the state in the interest of Central relation towards foreign states and public order for preventing incitement and commission of any kind of cognizable crime.

Shreya Singhal Vs Union of India

The fact of the case is a cartoonist was denied for making a cartoon. Who is from West Bengal arrested for drawing a particular cartoon based on Chief Minister and posted it on internet and also the persons work like this post more than 2 women has been arrested in this case there was a fight against section 66A of Information Technology Act which prohibits sharing any offensive information's in online the supreme court took this case on the ground of violating article 19(1)(a) most probably did not pass reasonable restriction also[17]. The argument under the case is to protect the public order where as the issue under section 66A is also causing a chilling effect towards the speech and expression which has been addressed by the court the chilling effect on free speech has its fail to give the proper definition towards them offensive inconvenience 66A. As the result suction 66a of Information Technology Act 2000 was completely struck down as it was violated article 19 one of the Constitution of India[18].

Various Reports of Internet Censorship in India

In our country most preventive methods to access online or internet content take place under section 69(a) of Information Technology Act 2000 which also direct the government to stop or block harmful contents which can be either about the state or about any of the protestations by the public or to protect the interest of sovereignty and integrity of a country[19]. Internal censorship in our country can have a sudden shutdown of Internet in various state by using URL blocking as well as a complete shutdown of websites.

- Reporters without borders:- it is a set of list of reporters without borders, under this list of countries which are serve lens from March 2012 for example the instant took place on Mumbai for bombing the year 2008 by which India was added to this list of current Enemies under internet in the year 2014 and it is also still being a part of this Particular list.
- Open Net Initiative Report:- in this particular report India engage as a selective for the internet filtering post or any other material related to political conflict security purpose and social or IT act as a internet tool from 2011 and has been censored for such content it also has some set of rules and conditions that to block by country it has to be a vast portion of content in various country most probably the category should be able

to figure it out from medium level filtering or from numerous categories the selective few specific sides are being blocked or it can be small number of category also which comes under the targeted classification even though when there is no evidence the website still being blocked by the government.

- Freedom House Report:-Freedom house report stated India as one of the freedom on net status for party leafy with the rating 41Declared on 2016 which is better than lower This limit on the content was based on the protection of violence and for uses right in that particular report India was ranked 29th country out of 65 countries in this report.

Pros and Cons of Internet Censorship in India

The prone of internet sensation helps in eliminating miss information messages that creative enmity in the society especially about fake news rumors which is unwanted and also any kind of controversial matters related to state or politics which creates a Bias in society. In a positive role it helps in security of individual privacy business and transaction it also else in place is called dark web where many illegal activities are available, it is very necessary to protect the private information's of every individual and business the personal data of every individual should be very secured then it can be done only by internet censorship. The regulations by government towards internet censorship can easily make any kind of provision and long that should be followed by each and every individual or else it could lead to Penalty[20].

The disadvantage of internet censorship are where a set of rules and regulation get overpower towards authority and only some set of people being authorized to control censorship towards internet for their own benefit it act as arbitrary in nature, In reality internet censorship is very expensive many country faces it fortune. The information which has been controlled according to the survey done by economic forum it is common that one out of 4 people in overall world are using the internet but many people are facing penalties just because of online content And many nations have strict loss respect to internet Censorship Which is against Rights and freedom of individual.

Suggestions

It is observe that in Civil Society organisation individuals are facing penalties but the authorities for the usage of censored internet this is acid that bring when an actual content in internet site is been blocking which is inconsistently up Pride throat the communication or information many research suggest that there is only 27.64% of blog website that are officially blocked rest of others are unofficially blocked. The freedom of speech and expression is a medium which include reasonable restrictions also that internet censorship as a restart the restriction it should be taken seriously by the government while implementing it.

That every situations who gives his genuine opinion about politics or other contribution topic should not be prosecuted the blocks post which are genuine and has true content with the actual research made should not be taken down or struck down just an act of violating the freedom of speech and expression in India that doesn't mean the government cannot have criteria or sensor free speech and flow of information it can be held moreover the government should also handle the requested made towards internet censorship law properly seeing its advantage and disadvantage and tackle the hassle.

Conclusion

The government should handle internet censorship with the right balance between freedom of speech and expression and including other components as far as internet censorship as being quite in inadequate in terms of politics and business management regarding freedom of expression speech by blocking content for the benefit of politics and personal information is also a variation of speech and expression so the law should be very transparent enough that every citizen understand properly and that they should be certain change which has to be followed by government also so that there is a balance between internet censorship and freedom of speech and expression.

CHAPTER SIX

RIGHT TO PROTEST, ITS LIMITATIONS AND RESPONSIBILITIES

Author: Abhishek Parmar, III year of B.A.,LL.B.(Hons.) from Jagran Lakecity University, Bhopal

People's voices are important. They have the right to express themselves, share information, and call for a better world. They also have the right to agree or disagree with those in power and to peacefully oppose their views. Living in an open and fair society, where people can seek justice and enjoy their human rights, requires exercising these rights without fear or unlawful interference.

Dr. Martin Luther King Jr has rightly said that - "The ultimate tragedy is not the oppression and cruelty by the bad people but the silence over that by the good people."[i]

In a well-ordered society, every individual has a prima facie obligation to obey the law and to oppose or protest laws that are incompatible with the citizen's fundamental rights.

A protest is a gathering of people who come together to openly express their feelings about a social issue. Protests against the Citizenship (Amendment) Act (CAA) of 2019 at Delhi's Shaheen Bagh or farmers' year-long protest against the three farm laws from 2020 to 2021 are examples of recent protests across the country. The right to peaceful protest is guaranteed by India's constitution. In this post, we'll look at the Constitutional Right to Protest, its limitations, its importance, and various Supreme Court rulings on the subject. [ii]

<u>Introduction</u>

Fundamental Rights are guaranteed in Part III of the Indian Constitution. The Supreme Court hasconstrued the freedoms protected by Part III of the constitution in several rulings. The goal was to put citizens in the driver's seat and hold the government accountable.

The seeds of protest, such as satyagraha, were sowed deep during India's independence movement, making protest a vital and indelible chapter in the country's history, leading constitutional writers to conclude that the right to protest is an essential aspect of human life.

The right to protest, to publicly criticize the government and attempt to persuade it to respond, is a fundamental political right of the people that arise directly from a democratic interpretation of different parts of Article 19. Although the Right to Protest is not expressly stated in the Fundamental Rights, it can be inferred from Article 19's Right to Freedom of Expression and Speech.

Right to Freedom of Speech – Article 19(1)(a)

The right to free speech and expression entails the ability to publicly express one's views on government actions.

Right to Freedom of Association- Article 19(1)(b)

The ability to build political organizations is essential. These can be organizedto raise collective objections to government actions.

Right to Freedom of Assembly – Article 19(1)(c)

Individuals have the right to peacefully assemble to question and object to government activities through demonstrations, agitations, and public assemblies, as well as to organize long-term protest movements.

People's right to protest means that they can function as watchdogs and constantly scrutinize the actions of governments. It gives governments feedback on their policies and actions, after which the concerned government identifies and corrects its mistakes through consultation, meetings, and discussion.

When these rights are united, anybody can peacefully congregate and demonstrate against the government's actions or inactions. The demonstrations are in support of democracy, with the goal of protecting the integrity of the country's flaws.

Under the strong leadership of Babasaheb Ambedkar, the authors of the Constitution put their hearts and minds into writing an inclusive Constitution for a varied India. As chairman of the Drafting Committee, Ambedkar was crystal clear on one point: the Constitution's purpose. He stated, "the Constitution is not a mere lawyer's document; it is a vehicle of life and its spirit is always the spirit of the age".

The fact that our Constitution balances citizens' rights and responsibilities is one of its most important features. These are societal constructs that have evolved over time, via tradition, and through use. The Constitution's citizens' obligations are essentially a codification of tasks that are fundamental to the Indian way of life, focusing on tolerance, peace, and communal harmony. A detailed examination of Article 51A's clauses reveals that several of them pertain to principles that have long been a part of Indian mythology, religion, and traditions.

The Constitution's Fundamental Rights chapter recognizes the importance of obligations. One is the right to free speech; however, Clauses 2 to 6 of Article 19 provide for reasonable limitations on the use of such rights. This means that when exercising one's rights, one must keep in mind one's responsibilities to these constitutional ideals.

Today, it is vital to stress the necessity of remembering our constitutional responsibilities for the sake of our country's growth. Democracy will not be able to take root in society unless citizens strike a balance between their natural rights and their basic responsibilities.

Restriction[iii] on Right to Protest

The right to freedom of speech and expression is subject to reasonable restrictions under Article 19(2). These reasonable restrictions are in place for the following reasons:

Sovereignty and integrity of India, Security of the State, friendly relations with foreign States,Public order, Decency or morality, Contempt of court, Defamation, and Incitement to an offense. Further, resorting to violence during the protest is a violation of a key fundamental duty of citizens.Enumerated in Article 51A, the Constitution makes it a fundamental duty of every citizen "to safeguard public property and to abjure violence".

Importance of Right to Protest for Democracy

The active exercise of one's right to protest ensures that citizens function as watchdogs, always scrutinizing the government's acts and ensuring that they are carried out fairly.

The protests have significance because:

- Protests have traditionally sparked positive social change and the progress of human rights, and they serve to encourage the identification and defense of civic space around the world.

- Human Rights Advancement: Protests encourage citizens to become more involved and aware.
- Contributing to all sectors of life: Protests play an important role in civic, political, economic, social, and cultural life in all societies.
- Empowers Marginalized Groups: This is especially important for persons whose interests are neglected or ignored in other ways.
- Strengthen Democracy: They aid in the promotion of representative democracy by permitting direct participation in public affairs.
- Increases Accountability: They enable individuals and organizations to express their dissatisfaction and complaints, communicate ideas and opinions, expose governance flaws, and publicly demand that governments and other powerful institutions address issues and hold themselves accountable for their actions.

Supreme Court's Judgements on the Right to Protest

The Supreme Court stated that while "democracy and dissent go hand in hand," "demonstrations expressing disagreement must be held only in specified venues." The Constitution protects the right to demonstrate and voice opposition, but it is accompanied by Fundamental Duties such as Article 51A, which declares that every citizen has a fundamental responsibility to defend public property and refrain from violence.

Judgements[iv]

In Himat Lal K. Shah v. Commissioner of Police, Ahmedabad & Anr. (1972), the rights provided under Section 33(1)(o) of the Bombay Police Act, 1951 were used to challenge the Commissioner of Police, Ahmedabad's rules. Before having public meetings, one of these restrictions required that prior authorization be acquired. The Supreme Court concluded that the state can only pass laws that promote each citizen's freedom to assemble and that reasonable limits can only be imposed for the sake of public order. The freedom to hold meetings on public streets was subject to the control of the relevant authorities over the time and venue of the meeting, as well as issues of public order, in evaluating whether these rules infringed Article 19(1)(b) of the Indian Constitution.

Ramlila Maidan Incident vs. Union of India's Home Secretary (2012)[v]: Citizens have a fundamental right to peacefully congregate and demonstrate, according to the Supreme Court, which cannot be taken away by arbitrary administrative or legislative action.

The Supreme Court of India held in Beenu Rawat v. Union of India (2013) that rights and obligations must be balanced. While everyone has the right to criticize unjust government action, protesting against police activity (or inaction) is particularly risky since fundamental rights are more likely to be infringed. At the same time, protesters were unable to bring the state's machinery to a halt. People had the freedom to demonstrate, but they also had a responsibility to follow the law. The role of the police was to keep peace. In this sense, there must be a balance because "rights without responsibilities tend to develop into a license for the misuse of rights."

In another decision, Anita Thakur v. the State of J&K (2016), the Supreme Court ruled that there is a basic right to protest and organize peaceful assemblies using freedom of speech and expression. Force could only be used to disperse these assemblies if they became illegal. The Court did warn, however, that the use of force must be reasonable and not excessive.

Mazdoor Kisan Shakti Sangathan v. Union of India & Anr. was cited in the Shaheen Bagh decision (2018) The key point of argument here was whether the resulting disturbances to residents were a wider public interest for which the freedom to protest in that location might be limited. There had to be a balance between everyone's rights. In this case, the court determined that the contested demonstration was causing substantial harassment to the residents. Simultaneously, the protest site, Jantar Mantar, was a regular spot for protests and was also recognized by the authorities. As a result, the Court ordered the authorities to develop suitable and necessary standards for regulating protests in the region.

The court upheld the right to peaceful protest against laws in the Shaheen Bagh decision of 2019 but clarified that public roadways and public areas cannot be occupied indefinitely. Fundamental freedoms do not exist in a vacuum. The protestor's right must be balanced against the commuter's right, and both must coexist in mutual respect.

In Anuradha Bhasin v. Union of India (2020), the Supreme Court distinguished between "law and order" and "public order," stating that public order limitations require a higher bar for activation. A minor annoyance cannot be considered a credible threat to the public's safety. However, the Court did not explain why the inconvenience was a proper premise for reasonable limits to be implemented in this case.

Conclusion

"When it gets down to having to use violence, then you are playing the system's game. The establishment will irritate you – pull your beard, flick your face – to make you fight. Because once they've got you violent, then they know how to handle you. The only thing they don't know how to handle is non-violence and humor."— John Lennon

Protesting against injustice is not only a fundamental right provided by the Indian Constitution, but it is also a moral obligation. By now, we've established that the right to protest is protected by the constitution. It is regarded as 'precious' in some cases to secure the right to free expression and peaceful protest, and it should be maintained in all circumstances. However, these rights are not absolute in nature and should be subjected to reasonable constraints, as stipulated under Article 19(2), which is critical in the interests of the country's sovereignty and integrity. Fundamental rights do not exist in a vacuum, and the rights of protestors and commuters should be balanced. The court's main point is that peaceful protest is a basic right of protestors and should be tolerated. However, if a protest infringes on the rights of others, generating serious concerns for the general public, such as the possibility of a blockade, discomfort, or a protest that interrupts daily life, the right to protest can be prohibited.

CHAPTER SEVEN

CRIMINOLOGY AND CRIMINAL LAW

Author: Aparna Kumari, I year of B.Com.,LL.B. from Institute of Law Nirma University

Crime is unavoidable in human society as the violation of the code of conduct prescribed for the harmony of human society is bound to occur. Crime is a condition that is ever-present. An increase in restrictions and sanctions increases the evil. The more the development of human society, the more frequent the human failure. The different groups have got different interests in the society, which leads to conflicts that eventually result in a crime.

Crimes are immoral and harmful acts for the general public or human society. The changing concept of the crime depends on human evolution all over the world. That is why different countries have got different laws to tackle different types of crying. What is legal in one country may be illegal in another.

The legal frame of crime is – a " revolution of the form of conduct which is declared to be socially and legally unpleasant and it's forbidden by law with some punishment ". An individual who has committed a certain legal action is a criminal. There are certain components like - intention, a voluntary act, competent age, degree of intent, and legal injury, that must be there in order to deal with an individual as a criminal.

CHARACTERISTICS OF A CRIME

There are certain characteristics that make an act unlawful and are forbidden and punishable under a legal framework. They are:-

- Actus reus - an act forbidden by law must be performed.

- Mens-rea - one must have a guilty mind that is intended to cause harm is important.
- Bad consequences - the crime performed should have caused harm to a group, society, state, or an individual mentally, physically, or emotionally.
- Prohibited under the law - The act must be forbidden under the existing law.
- Punishable - the act in order to be considered a crime must not only be prohibited but punishable under the penal law as well.

Criminology is the scientific study of crime and criminals and the motivation behind such harmful behaviors. This helps in understanding the criminal mind, the reason behind such at, and the prevention of crime through the development of law in the state. Criminology includes the process of making laws, breaking laws, and punishment for breaking the laws. The practical role of criminology is to form and impact social and legal policies.

According to criminologists fear, want of Revenge, a certain passion, obsession, or any kind of interest in criminals lead to crime in society. No child sets foot in life as an offender. It's a gradual process by which a child develops the personality of a thief, kidnapper, burglar, robber, etc whatever task fascinates them. The behavior of humans is unenforceable as they are free to choose the course they wish to go after. But criminology attempts to deal with human behavior that is relevant due to the environmental factors, genes, societal impacts, and habits to conduct a crime.

Criminology is concerned with the source of crime and contains

(i) criminal biology that informs the reason for the criminal mind to be found in the mental and physical composition of the offender such as Hereditary likelihood and physical defects.

(ii) criminal sociology, which bargains with the effect of upbringing environment such as the root cause of malefaction.

Criminologists look at a number of linked topics, such as:

- People who commit crimes have certain characteristics.
- Crimes are committed for a variety of reasons.
- Individual and community effects of crime.
- Crime-prevention techniques.

Criminologists have expanded the definition of crime to encompass behavior that is not illegal. Economic exploitation, racial discrimination, and hazardous or unhealthy working conditions are all examples of this.

Criminal law is a set of rules laid down by a state to reflect civilization, moral values, political setup, public knowledge, and respect for others' rights. Criminal law also sets the ground of punishment for the conflicts resulting out due to offenses. Criminal law sets the procedure for the investigation, trial, and punishment of the offender. Different types of crime have been defined under criminal law with punishment for them.

Depending on how people perceive it, criminal law serves a variety of purposes. Criminal law serves a variety of purposes, including keeping criminals out of society, assisting in their rehabilitation, and punishing offenders. However, the two primary purposes of criminal law are to teach society what is morally acceptable and wrong and to punish those who transgress the law.

Criminal law originated from the dispute to different interests of different groups in the society. Violation of the status of interest of one group by the other leads to conflict which ultimately causes crime. Criminal law secures these interests and provides protection from violation of individuals' enjoyment of life .

CHAPTER EIGHT

JUDICIAL INTERVENTION IN ARBITRATION PROCEEDINGS

Author: Shiwanjali Tripathi, V year of B.B.A.,LL.B. from New Law College, Bharati Vidyapeeth University, Pune.

INTRODUCTION

Arbitration law is based on the notion of removing a dispute from the usual courts and allowing the parties to choose a domestic body to resolve it. It should come as no surprise that arbitration, unlike other administrative adjudications, does not take place entirely on its own, but does come under court jurisdiction at some point. With the goal of resolving disputes quickly, it is critical that arbitration cases be determined only on the basis of affidavits and other relevant papers, rather than on the basis of oral evidence.

SCOPE OF JUDICIAL INTERVENTION

Despite the fact that arbitration is a distinct method for resolving a dispute, the courts have the authority to intervene in the proceedings under the Arbitration and Conciliation Act, 1996. The Act aimed to divert cases from the traditional route of litigation to arbitration, so legislators included provisions to limit time-consuming judicial intervention and allowing speedy resolution. There are three types of court intervention in arbitration:-

- Section 5 of the 1996 Act (prior to proceedings)
- Section 9 of the 1996 Act- During the course of the proceedings
- Following the processes, in terms of arbitral awards

JUDICIAL INTERVENTION BEFORE ARBITRATION PROCEEDINGS

Section 5 of the Arbitration and Conciliation Act of 1996 specifies the scope of court action. This part is strikingly similar to Article 5 of the UNCITRAL Model Law. It clearly intended for Section 5 of the Act to limit the involvement of the Court in arbitration. In order to fulfill the twin goals of expedited justice and cost-effective conflict settlement, parties are allowed to control court's intervention. It eliminates the prospect of judicial intervention. The wording "no judicial power" is broad enough, and the Act additionally assures that there is no judicial discretion involved by employing the verb "must interfere". The duty of the judiciary is purely administrative, not judicial.

JUDICIAL INTERVENTION DURING PROCEEDINGS

The act's section 9 deals with the court's ability to give interim measures. Section 17 gives arbitral tribunals the authority to make orders in accordance with the section. While Section 9 has the same authority as the Judiciary, the two sections serve fundamentally different purposes. The power granted in Section 9 is mandatory and not subject to the autonomy of the parties in dispute. Section 9 application is not a civil matter. The court's role is confined to ensuring that an arbitral panel's rights to adjudication are not violated. One of the issues with Section 17 is the lack of an appropriate legislative framework in the Act itself for the execution of interim orders of the arbitral tribunal.

JUDICIAL INTERVENTION AFTER PROCEEDINGS

The application for setting aside the arbitral award is described in Section 34 of the Act. It states that judicial involvement is prohibited, but it also explains the exceptions to this rule, such as when an arbitral award can be set aside by a court. Section 34(2)(a) states that the courts may set aside an arbitral judgement if:

The arbitration agreement is not legitimate under the law to which the parties to the agreement were subjected, and the party was incapacitated, the arbitrator's appointment or the proceedings were not properly announced, the case was not one that could be referred to arbitration, or the award contained a decision that was outside the scope of the arbitration, the tribunal's composition did not follow the parties' agreement, the arbitration agreement is not valid under the law to which it was subjected by the parties to the agreement etc.

The courts may also set aside an award under Section 34(2)(b) of the Act if the subject matter of the dispute cannot be resolved through arbitration or the arbitral award is contrary to Indian public policy. The grounds set forth in section 34(2)(a) are so narrow that the courts are unable to intervene in arbitral judgements. The only confusing phrase in this section is the phrase "Indian public policy." It leaves itself open to interpretation, resulting in court involvement.

IS JUDICIAL INTERVENTION IN ARBITRATION JUSTIFIED ?

If a disagreement emerges, the court will refer the parties to an arbitration panel or bench before intervening. The government and related agencies are simply turned into antagonistic parties. The center's arbitrators are government employees who may be biased in favour of one party or the other for a variety of reasons. Politics, power, and money are all tools that can be used to purchase justice.

Arbitration proceedings are more informal, and arbitrators are often inexperienced with them. The majority of Arbitrators appointed by the Courts under Section 11 of the Act are retired judges who rely on long-standing procedures and submissions, resulting in a lengthy and grueling process akin to that of court proceedings. As a result, arbitration entails issues, oral and documentary evidence, chief and cross-examination, and other procedures. Hence, Court intervention to preserve a party's right, in administering justice is JUSTIFIED.

CONCLUSION

Therefore, under the circumstances, judicial action is necessary. However, judicial intrusion dilutes arbitration's basic goal and objective, necessitating a middle-ground approach, which can be achieved with a sufficient number of competent, trained, and honest arbitrators and well-equipped arbitral institutions which is important for the future success of arbitration in India. If there is a rising perception that choosing arbitration over litigation reduces the chances of achieving high-quality justice, arbitration's future is bleak.

CHAPTER NINE

APPLE INC. v. APPLE MAN

Author: Vamika Wadhwa, V year of B.A.,LL.B. from Maharaja Agrasen Institute of Management Studies, IPU

Apple Inc., a well-known brand, has always been in the news. In December 2021, Apple Inc. filed a notice of opposition against the movie Apple Man. Apple Man is a short Ukrainian film that is based on a superhero who can aloft apples in the air. The question thus arises: why has Apple Inc. filed a notice of opposition against this film? This article answers this question and discusses class 9 (International classes) of the trademark. Later, it focuses on the possible legal remedies available to the parties.

On November 22nd,2020, Vasyl Moskaltheno, the director, applied for a trademark under class 9 in the U.S Patent and Trademark Office. He wanted to protect the film and the devices used in it. After various extensions granted to the company (Acc. To section 13 of U.S Trademark law), on the 6th December 2021, Apple filed a notice of opposition against the registration of this trademark.

The notice mentions two issues; the first is that the registration of movies may cause consumer confusion, which is a violation of Section 2(d) of the Lanham Act. A trademark's main objective is to distinguish between the goods and services of one seller and another and it helps to differentiate between the products. The notice also stated that, though the name of the movie consists of the word "man", Apple Inc. is so famous and instantly recognizable that the similarities in both these trademarks might cause the ordinary consumer to believe that the movie is related to, affiliated with, or endorsed by Apple. Another point is that Apple has many terms, such as Apple TV, Apple Music, Apple News, etc., which can also lead to consumers thinking that the applicant's mark is a further extension of Apple. Apple in the past has offered various services offering similar kinds of products, such as gaming, e-books, video-on-demand, films, etc. This can deceive the consumer.

The second ground mentioned by the company is regarding the dilution of a famous mark. The well-known trademark states that it is the kind of trademark that a segment of society is aware of. Apple Inc. fits into this definition properly. The company gives proper evidence through various surveys conducted by Forbes, Microsoft, and Spectrum Enterprises regarding the trademark being a well-known trademark. These surveys showed that Apple has been at the top of the list and hence it is one of the world's most famous brands. Apple also makes the statement that it will damage the reputation of the mark and that it can cause dilution in the minds of consumers. This is a violation of Section 43 of the United States Trademark Act. The company also views that the applicant's mark is similar in appearance, meaning, and impression with regards to the apple mark, and if the registration is granted, apple will also be able to use the applicant's mark inference to the prima facie of the case.

Vasyl Monskaleno has not issued a written statement, but he has made it clear through media that he prefers to resolve the matter through negotiation rather than litigation. Even though, both the parties are engaged in negotiations and have requested the court for an extension which was granted by the court. Both the products fall under class 9 of the trademark. This class focuses on various categories such as computer software, apparatus, and instruments for scientific research in laboratories, safety equipment, cinematography cameras, cinematographic films, etc. The US Patent and Trademark office divides 45 different classes of products and services. The purpose of these classes is to help the applicant avoid trademark objections in the future and allow smooth and streamlined registration of the mark. In this particular case, the products are different from one another, yet the description of the class of trademark falls into both categories. Therefore, in my view, it can be a reason to create confusion in the minds of consumers.

As stated above, Apple Inc. talks about the confusion that might arise due to the name of the movie. This confusion isn't related to the name but arose because of the registration of both the products in the same class. As stated above, class 9 covers various categories. These categories are different from each other, as seen in this case, where Apple Inc. covers the articles related to computer software. On the other hand, a movie seeks registration for cinematographic equipment and film. In my view, these two are very different categories, clubbed together in a particular class. Hence, to reduce confusion this particular class should be subdivided for the smooth functioning of trademark registration.

Apple Inc. mentions Section 43 of US Trademark Law in its notice of opposition, which discusses dilution by blurring and mentions a few factors such as the degree of similarity between the mark and the mark, the degree of recognition of the mark, and the user's intention to associate with a famous mark. But there are some exceptions. This case is a perfect example of an exception. According to the facts of this case, it might seem to be a perfect example of dilution, but from my point of view, this case is an exception and hence is covered in section 43(3) (Exclusion) of the act. Apple is a very generic word that is used across the world. Even though it is a registered trademark, the movie describes the word differently, so I believe it is a fair use of the trademark.

In conclusion, it seems that Apple might have some valid points, but considering the mark used in the movie is completely different, it is fair use. Apple should be granted registration under sections 8 and 15 of the act. It should also be noted that Apple Man has suffered from damage to its reputation, and in my opinion, certain relief should be granted to the movie maker.

CHAPTER TEN

FREEDOM OF MEDIA: ISSUES AND CHALLENGES WITH SPECIAL REFERENCE TO MEDIA TRIALS BY SOCIAL MEDIA

Author: Dr.J.S.Chandpuri (LLM,UGCNET,PhD), Associate Professor Deptt. of Law DAV(PG) College Dehradun, Uttarakhand.

Introduction

In India, the freedom of media is one of the most important aspects for protection and nourishment of fundamental rights, which enshrined under our constitution. The media is a fundamental institution of society. It plays a very vital role in creating, shaping and reflecting the public. Opinion in a democracy, it establishes, to direct communication between the people and the government. The acts of media is just like a bridge, between the govt. and the people. The media is rightly described as the fourth pillar of the state. But the media can play an effective role only, when if media is free to express its views and articulate its opinion. As air is to life so also freedom of media, without air no life can survive. So also without freedom, no media can exist to play a significant role in all democratic countries of the world, the right to freedom of media is regarded as the very foundation and the indispensable condition for the existence of every other rights. Article 19(1) a) of Indian constitution secures to all its citizen the 'right to freedom of speech and expression' unlike the U.S. Constitutional provisions, there is no separate provisions guaranteeing freedom of the media in India. It may be pointed out that the word expression in Article19(1)(a) is used in addition to the word speech and thus is comprehensive enough to cover freedomofMedia, in fact, a number of cases, the supreme court has held that the term freedom of speech and expression includes the freedom of media, absence of a specific mention of freedom of press in the constitution created no difficulty when the court was called upon to protect the freedom in the celebrated case of RomeshThappar V. State of Madras.[1] The Supreme Court has no doubt in propounding that freedom of speech and expression included 'Freedom of propagation of ideas, and that the freedom of circulation, the court held that liberty of circulation was an essential to the freedom as the 'liberty of publication'. In this way, the learned judge clarified that freedom of expression included that freedom of propagation of ideas, their publication and circulation. Justice PatanajaliSastri former judge of supreme court had observed that the freedom of media is an 'essential part' of the right to freedom of speech and expression as declared under Art. 19(1)(a) of the constitution.[2] 'In Re Harijai Singh[3] Hon'ble Mr. Justice Faizan Uddin of the supreme court observed that the freedom of media was a part of the speech and expression declared under Article 19(1)(a) of the constitution and thus, the freedom of media was included in the freedom of expression.

Media plays a significant role in society, therefore freedom of media has become indispensable for civil society. In democratic governance system media works as a bridge between public and govt. media is bringing dynamic changes in society through its communication. The contribution of the media cannot be forgotten in the field of people's living standard i.e. eating habits, education, employment, working pattern, business management and style of living etc. Media make community aware through its information and communications in this regard media acts like a 'watch full dog' in society. Media has a reach in all parts of society, whether it is print media, newspaper, magazines or broad casting media, radio, doordarshan, computer or social media i.e. facebook, whatsapp, twitter, email, YouTube and many other apps, are directly connected with society, it has become an integral part of community. Media is the sword arm of democracy, it protect public interest against malpractice and create public awareness. Today when politicians are taking full advantage of their positions, an evil nexus of mafia and crime syndicate is making the life of siphoned out for the personal gain of the influential, and ordinary people are most spectator, media has a greater responsibility to expose such malpractice of concerned person.[4]

<u>Social Media and its significance in Society</u>

Social Media means websites and applications that enable users to create and share content or to participate in social networking[5] such as Google, Facebook, Twitter, Instagram, WhatsApp, Wikipedia, YouTube and other commercial sites etc.

In today's society, the use of social media has been a necessary daily activity. Social media is typically used for social interaction and access to news and information, and decision making. It is a valuable communication tool with others locally and worldwide, as well as to share, create and spread information. The recent development in wireless technology have introduced new means and directions of communication, million of people all over the world are now engaged in political, economic cultural and educational discourses due to the vast expansion of the world wide web. Indeed, Social media has transformed people' lifestyles and has introduced a new pattern of social interaction.[6] According an estimate more than 67% of internet users are engaged on Facebook and You Tube. As of the first quarter of 2019, twitter averaged 332 million monthly active users, while the Instagram has become the 4th most downloaded mobile app of the world.[7] TheWhatsApp has become the world's most popular messaging application by 2015-16[8] and has over 2.9 billion users worldwide as of February 2022. It has become the primary means of electronic communication in multiple countries and locations, including Latin America, the Indian subcontinent and large parts of Europe and Africa.[9]YouTube is the second most-visited website after Google search, according to Alexa interent rankings. YouTube allows users to upload, view, rate, share and to playlists, report, comment on videos and subscribe to other users. "Socialmedia plays a vital role in todays' social life, it isa web-based online tools that enable to people discover and learn new information, share ideas, interact with new people and organizations. More than 46% of people spent 30% of their time in social networking platforms. Nowadays more than 86% of all business have a dedicated to social media platforms as part of their marketing strategy. Almost 60% of marketers are devoting the equivalent of a full work day to social media marketing for development and maintenance. Social media has quickly entered the educational field, it has also introduced online learning, which is becoming more popular among students all over the world.[10] Overall social media can be considered as a foundational shift in daily activities and lifestyles. It is also a step toward a new communication environment.

Media Trials by Social Media – The term trial means and includes that any decision of a court in respect of any suit or proceedings on the basis of sufficient evidence. Trial primarily denotes the function of judiciary, by which they dispose out the fact in issue of parties of the suit. But nowadays this work is being done by broad casting media, print media as well as social media.

In the blind race of TRP the media has ignored the real or true fact, and only distorting imaginary facts are being presented before the viewers. "Social Media trial is wherein the individuals themselves do a separate investigation of facts and form public opinion against the accused even before the court takes cognizance of the case, it creates prejudices in the public and sometimes even judges".

Social Media trial is a phrase describing by various social media appliances, such as Facebook, Youtube, WhatsApp, Twitter, Instagram etc. coverage on a case through an attempt by such media to hold the accused guilty even before the trials begin in competent court. "The Social Media usually portrays the accuses a villain not based on facts but only to sensationalize the news, which causes damage to the dignity of the accused. Media through their trail attempts to reincarnate itself into a public court and interfere with court proceedings. It fails to analyze the vital gap between on accused and a convict keeping at stake the golden principles of 'presumption of innocence until proven guilty' and guilt beyond reasonable doubt'.[11]

Not only in personal matter of an individual but also in matter of public importance or public interest social media acts unilaterally in haste without sufficient evidence, which can be very harmful or derogatory to the unity and integrity of the nation. For example, recently, in Banaras, without disclosure of the report of enquiry commission on Gyanvapi mosque, various social media sites had given their verdict, as a result of which Hindu-Muslim organizations as well as the entire country facing the environment of anarchy, a part from this various social media are working to get support to public opinion through online, infavour and disfavour of Mandir-Masjid, whch is not a good sign for the unity and integrity of the country. The case of murder of his mother by a 16 years old boy in Lucknow, is making headlines these days on Social media. Everyday a new facts are coming out in this incident. In the initial days, the media had come to conclusion that the accused boy used to play PUBG and his mother had scolded him hence he did so out of anger. But later stories depict the illicit relationship of the deceased with someone else. Whatever be the case, the character of a person cannot be revealed publicity among the people. This is just against to the dignity of deceased person. No vice journalists or who do not know the law, interfering in the personal matter of people, make them prime news of social media and themselves appear in the role of judge only for the fame of name. Not only this, they create pressure on people for reporting under the privileges assumed by themselves.

In the celebrated case of R. Raj Gopal Vs State of Tamil Nadu[12] popularly known as 'Auto Shanker Case' the supreme court has expressly held that 'Right to privacy' or the right to be let alone is guaranteed by Article 21 of the constitution. A Citizen has right to safeguard the privacy of his own, his family, marriage, procreation, motherhood, child bearing and education among other matters. None can publish anything concerning the above matters without his consent, whether truthful or otherwise and whether laudatory or critical. If he does so, he would be violating the right of the person concerned and would be liable in an action for damage, further the court has emphasized that the following cases, viz. a female who is the victim of a sexual assault, kidnapping abduction or a like offences should not further be subjected to the indignity of her name or her photographs and such incident should not published in media.[13] The Social Media trial is an intrusion and an ethical breach as well as an invasion on right to privacy. Recently, a news was circulated on Facebook, in which a 50 years old man is married to a 25 years old girl, they are brutally persecuted and harassed by social media. This incident is just an example. Nowadays hundreds of such incidents are prevalent on social media, and the administration is sitting as silent. It has become a trend that social media performs the function of the judiciary of investigating the truth. But the media mostly fails to bring out the truth and takes its decision only on the basis of presupposition.

'Families and relatives of people accused of crimes have recently used the influence of social media to reopen proceedings. In the cases of the murder of Jessica Lal, PriyaDarshaniMattoo, NitishKatara, BMW and Aarushi murder, media influence was observed in full swing. In 2015, A Delhi Women, Jasleen Kaur, posted a photo of a man, Sarvjeet Singh on facebook and accused him of sexual harassment. The facebook post went viral which was followed by a media trial labeling the man a 'pervert', Delhi kadarinda (The Delhi's predator). Four years later, the man was later found out to be innocent by the Delhi Court and was acquitted of all the charges. The widespread use of social media influence the legal process. More importantly the regular usage of platforms such as twitter and Facebook represent threats to the fair trial ideal.[14]

Article 19(1)(a) of the constitution guarantees to all citizen 'the right to freedom of speech and expression. Clause (2) of this article, at the same time provides some restriction on this rights, the freedom of speech and expression is not an absolute right and restriction can be imposed under sovereignty and integrity of India, the security of state friendly relations with foreign states, public order, decency or morality or relation to contempt of court, defamation or incitement to an offence. It maystated that the exercise of right conferred by Article 19(1)(a) carries special duties and responsibilities.[15] Section 2 of the contempt of Court Act 1971 interference in the administration of justice specifically referred to as contempt in the definition of criminal contempt. Social Media reporting is inadmissible evidence and putting it into the public domain, the media draws the judge's attention to details that are not to be addressed in adjudicating the case and could subconsciously influence the judge's judgement under our legal system, a suspect/accused has the right to a fair trial and is presumed to be innocent until proven guilty in a court of law. Thus their prejudices emerge as a vice to society that is influences public minds. Sometimes the social media presents the judgement passed by the court in the form of social debates for making them to criticism of public. The most famous example is the Km Nanavati case[16] where the public opinion affected the conviction of the accused.

Impact of Media trial on Legal System

Social Media mostly takes the decision without properly knowing the facts or truth of incident. Due to the thirst and hunger of name and fame, social media often reaches the conclusion hastily, which creates difficulties for the judicial process as well law and society. 'Trial' refers to the function of judiciary, it denotes a proceedings which is convened before the court and any decision would be taken by the court on the ground of sufficient evidence. This is an adjudicating process which only exercised by judiciary. The absence of any strict code of conduct, allows people on the social media platforms to be largely active in voicing opinions especially ones that may have an effective role in framing the opinions of others. Ideally, in a democratic society, it is healthy to have a functioning social media for citizens to be able to express opinions freely under the 'Freedom of speech and expression' clause. But in the age of prevalence existence of social media, the fact is that many of the news in social media may be paid, fabricated and false. Furthermore, these 'fictions' evidence cause defamation to persons who have been acquitted by the courts based on a legal trial and on the grounds of lack of proof beyond reasonable doubt. Because of social media defamation, the accused victims in these cases face difficulty in resurrecting their reputation in society, ultimately jeoparding their rights to dignified life, causing serve psychological and physical harm. Due to absence of cross examination and sufficient evidence, social media sometimes acts to favors for a particular person rather than entire incident of the matter. It may be possible in media trial, to benefit one person at the cost of another, which is against the principle of natural justice. In few years back the law commission report even suggested a law to tackle trial by media. Trial which unprecedently goes over social media can be a contempt of court and even defamation in certain cases. The commission suggested the prohibition of elements that can provide to be prejudicial towards the accused. Justice Sikari even remarked about hard it hits the case when the people on the media decide and publish. What should be the outcome of a case. Trial by social media on private matters of an individual is a violation of their right to privacy, which tarnishes their dignity and reputation in open society. Not only this, in the absence of reality, whatever it shown by media, people accept it as correct, as a result, it led to harm the unity and integrity of nation.

Conclusion and Suggestions

Social media has reached every facet of human activities and become integral part of society. Social media is playing its important role in the society. Social Media has positive impact as well as some negative consequence in society. The cry of 'fake news' has become common place and consumer confidence in even traditional media outlets has been significantly eroded. In blind race of TRP the media as well as social media has ignored the ethic and only distorting – imaginary facts are being presented before the viewers. The social media has become accustomed to taking unilateral decisions without scrutiny of facts and cross-examination, it creates prejudices in the public and sometimes even judges. Sometimes media creates doubt the integrity of the judge who delivered the judgement. The trend of social media trial adversely affects the reputation of a person accused of an offence, by its pre-trial publication. It leads to the gross violation of his right to a fair trial, adversely affects the witness and also subconsciously affects the judges and lawyers. Neither a vigilant media can take the place of independent and impartial judiciary, nor judiciary can take the place of free and impartial media. Both are indispensable for the smooth functioning of our democratic tradition and the press should in no way be allowed to jeopardize the functions of the court.

The social media must not forget the social responsibility thrust upon it by respecting the powers of the judiciary as well as the right and dignity of the people in the larger interest of democracy. It must not unduly interfere with the functions of the court, inviting contempt proceedings against the media. The social media must perform the responsibility of restoring and maintaining the faith of the people in the honorable judiciary by restraining itself from unwarranted prejudicial publication which interferes with the fair trial of the accused and the administration of justice. Apart from this, circulation of inaccurate, baseless, graceless, misleading or distorted material on social sites should be a punishable offence. Comment on caste, religion or community, disclosure on social sites should be generally avoided or should be punished. Social media should not show or write anything that would provoke or incite personal violence or injuring on the right to privacy. Paramount interest of state, society and rights of an individuals should not be jeopardized. Violation of right to privacy should be made an offence punishable under the Indian Penal Code.

Besides this a strong legislation is required, by which a reasonable restriction could be imposed on social media. Apart from this social awareness programs as negative impact on society should be organized by NGOs, Govt. and Academic institutions from time to time. The Govt. should constitute an empowered committee to monitor or watch on social media which should give its report to the govt. from time to time.

Printed by Libri Plureos GmbH in Hamburg,
Germany